Inspired

Hayley Milliner

BookLeaf Publishing

India | USA | UK

Presentation by *BookLeaf Publishing*

Web: www.bookleafpub.com

E-mail: info@bookleafpub.com

ISBN: 9789358736946

First edition 2023

*Matilda and Maddox always aim high anything
is possible.*

ACKNOWLEDGEMENT

I would like to acknowledge every body who has been on this journey so far with me.. for the love, support and enthusiasm from you all.

PREFACE

All of the experiences featured in this book are written from the heart and with love.

My worth

That day I woke things were not the same,
Something was different,
I can't give it a name.
That realisation to know my worth,
Life is a blessing not a curse.
From this day on I took control,
My story now must be told.

The skys got you

Don't forget to look up at the end of each day
Them Stars they shine for you in everyway
The Moon shines bright
A sign to stay alive
Those negative thoughts they take them away
You're worthy of every last one
It's never to late to start again
It hurts so bad they understand
Come along and hold my hand
What's there today is gone tomorrow
The pain you feel
The never ending sorrow
You can let go you don't have to be brave
The stars and Moon their safe that way
They won't judge
They'll hold on
They won't judge what's right or wrong
Hold on tight
Let it all take flight
You don't have to take it to tomorrow
Let your guard down
Leave behind your sorrow

Friends

Friends,
The people we choose,
The ones that we are afraid to lose.
But the ones that stay,
The ones we gain,
The wholesome humans along the way.
They build us up and make us strong,
They remind us daily where we belong.
They create the cherished memories,
Their a cut above the rest,
Their the ones that gain the title of 'ultimate and
Best'.
The people that keep you ground,
The ones that keep you strong,
And fill your life with happiness
And remind you where you belong.
Thankyou for your friendship,
For holding me so tight,
For reminding me everyday that I'm actually
doing alright.
Thankyou for the hugs,
For wiping away my tears,
When things go a little wrong and the odd
occasional cheers.
My favourite, special humans,

You my friends will see,
That for everyday you stick around,
You mean so much to me

The line of Life

5

You enter the world alone,
Where you join other souls,
To grow and make decisions for the end of
nowhere.
Every moment sketched in your memory
forever,
Like the greatest picture book of all time.
In this time we grow to love, hate, hurt, smile
and find happiness.
For some today,
For some it's too late.
What is the purpose??
The purpose is to be happy and content,
So one day when you close your eyes for the last
time.....
You know you've made it.

Change is a choice

Its never to late to say sorry,
It's never too late to say 'This isn't for me'
Or 'i want something different'.
With the change of seasons comes time,
This time is yours,
Spend it how you will
And make everyday count.
Just like the ones before.

Shes' Flawed

She's flawed,
Explored,
On the floor,
Ignored.
The words she speaks no longer adored.
The time she spent saying 'Hi I'm here',
Now just becomes another fear.
She's flawed,
Explored,
On the floor,
Ignored.
The touch of her hand no longer wanted,
Her wishes no longer granted,
Whilst they take an array of advantage.
She's flawed,
Explored,
On the floor,
Ignored.
No longer beautiful,
No longer wise,
No one desires to see what's inside.
She's flawed,
Explored,
On the floor,
Once ignored,
Once adored
And never sure.

Time

Imagine if clocks had a million hands,
One for everyone one of our plans.
All moving differently to all different times and
lands,
The on going ticking of those very hands.
Some can go back to the time you once lost,
Some going forward or even to stop.
One for the love that once got away,
The tears and the fears that you felt back that
day.
One for the death you didn't see coming,
Completely blind sided but cancer kept coming.
That birth where you missed that particular
person,
The joy and the pain of never knowing.
That time of the panic you would always be lost,
The one where you wanted to turn back the
clock.
The one of intense love that made you feel
weird,
Is this it for the rest of my years?
The time to go home when you don't want to
leave,
That one where you look right inside of me.

The one where you feel my heart beat in my
chest,
Forward to the one that holds the key to it all,
Where does this end in spite of it all?
The clock keeps on running the hands tick away,
But right now there's only two that are going that
way
Time is moving way to fast,
Putting yesterday right back firmly in the past.
Make the most of each moment cherish them all,
However big, however small.
Just know that I love you wherever you go,
When the hands stand still it's not time to go.
The memories are stuck deep in my head,
They go round and round when I'm laying in
bed.
There's a place in my heart especially for you,
A place where there's no clocks or hands made
for two.
It's warm and it's safe for when we are done.
The vivid memory of the joy along with the fun.
I'll keep it safe till my very last day,
When all of the memories will just float away.

It's war

I'm just a child
I know no politics or rules
I don't know what to do
I just know someone blew my house into two
Will you help me please?
No one answers my calls
I'm not taking liberties but these soldiers don't
play by the rules
I just know my family are gone
I'm just a child,
A child, I don't know how to be strong
Someone save me please!
I'm just a little person with needs
I am just a child
I know no politics or rules
I need someone to show me how to stand tall
To love me and guide me
So I can play by the rules

Just a child

I am a child,
As bright as can be,
Your SEN register doesn't define me.
I know things that my peers do not know,
But I may never be the star of the show.
Come into my world and see what I can do,
Don't always make me conform .
I'll show you!
I can name the planets, name all the dinosaurs,
I can tell you all the numbers without any pause.
I can lighten the life of anyone who goes by,
But sometimes I may come across as shy.
I'll be the kindest child you ever did meet,
But I may not understand your instructions and
sometimes never sleep.
Im happy in my world,
You should come and see.
Try living just for one day as me! .

Love yourself first always

Love has so many beautiful layers,
The way it makes you feel,
The way others feel,
And the love you can share.
Then there's the excitement,
It's not just one person or one memory,
But a place you can simply be.
It's an overwhelming fear of not living the
dream.
Don't wait for someone to love you.
It's ok to be alone.
Because deep down inside theres a love you get
to keep.
The feeling of self worth, confidence and
acceptance.
The one only you can really reach.
The very one that requires great patience and
alot of time.
The love deep down inside you,
The one you feel for you,
Is the best you can give someone and the worst
that you can lose.

It wasn't your time

Why couldn't you just stay and live some more
of life?
I needed you around some more,
I needed all of your advice.
That day when you were taken from right
underneath my nose,
I remember all the storm clouds and the constant
teary flows.
You had so much to live for,
So much more to do.
Life would of been so different because I really
needed you.
We look back on the good times,
The ones we love the best.
Noone talks about the day we laid you down to
rest.
Why do we lose the special ones? The ones with
all the soul?
The ones who are talented and wholesome,
Never get to grow old.
I feel like you were cheated,
The day you were taken from me,
And I will forever be angry,
That you didnt get to stay and live.

Sometimes it's hard

When a relationship is hard is it time to walk
away?
A multitude of questions coming straight your
way.
How well do you roll?
On an average day to day.
Are you the one of my dreams?
I'm tired of this feeling and constant low self
esteem.
Do you want me really? Or do I just fit right
now?
What is in the future and who really wears your
crown?
Is it really workable?
This thing of just you and me.
I was pretty sure love wasn't supposed to make
us feel so blue.
I don't want to run,
You know that thing that I always do,
But I just cannot get through to you.
Just say what you mean,
Don't just end the call,
I just need to know now once and for all.

The girl behind the curtain

The girl behind the curtain,
The one who copes all day and cries all night,
The one who smiles to everybody's face through
pain in broad day light.
She's the girl behind the curtain.
The one of fear and anxiety,
The one that leads her to pretend its ok when
she's down on bended knees.
The girl behind the curtain,
Shes always so happy and so bold,
But what happens to the happy bold girl
When it's dark and really cold.
The girl beneath the curtain who's something to
every one,
Sometimes the expectation are so high it's hard
to play along.
I'm ok ,it's ok, I'll do this or that,
But really she's so sad and down and sick of
feeling flat.
She laughs, she cries, she's sky high,
She's so down and she's so low,
She's the girl behind the curtain just going with
the flow.
Just remember what you see is not always what
you get,

No one shows their inner flaws or challenges
that they've met.
And the girl behind the curtain....
Just check that she's ok,
Because the girl behind the curtains had a really
awful day.

Time to heal

That whisper in the dark,
The secret tucked away way back in the past.
The void I chose to forget,
All the things I should have said.
'its not your fault'
'you'll be ok'
How can another human make you feel this
way?
I still remember it so clear,
The day you crossed the line and made me feel
fear.
Where was the protection?
I was supposed to feel so safe,
But you broke down all the barriers,
And only taught me how to hate.
I thought I'd blocked it all out,
My head so full of self doubt.
You ruined me that day,
When I watched my innocence float away.
The shaking and the tears,
The hurt that took away so many years.
This all just makes me who I am,
No one will ever get to take me down again.

My girl

She's a little a little baby girl,
A complete dream
And my whole world.
Eyes so brown for the world to see,
You'll never know how special you are to me.
Those chunky legs,
Great big smile,
That obvious personality that will change the
world in a while.
I can't wait to watch you grow in to all that you
can be,
We will have so much fun you and me.

She's a little girl stubborn as can be,
Those pig tails and beautiful face,
You're everything I dreamed.
So innocent and cheeky,
I've never felt so lucky,
Those curls and eyes of instant beauty,
You're even a little stroppy.
A solemn little soul
And everyday I live to watch you grow.
Your obvious creative flair,
The way you won't walk down the stairs.
You never sleep or rest to still,

But you my girl will climb the biggest hills.

She's a teen in her glory,
The moods next level and always full of stories.
Never do I ever forget the journey you've been
on,
The one that leads you to this very day and so
much further on.
You're absolutely stunning with so much more to
give,
You may not feel that you fit right now but you'll
see that's not so bad.
Your musical talent is endless,
The world is at your feet,
You are admirably dancing to your very own
beat.
Never ever lose that although you may lose your
way,
You have always known deep down what you
need to do this day.
You're a cloud of inspiration, individuality,
An aura of so much beauty that everyone around
you can see.
Always follow your heart the one that screams
right out,
The biggest dream you want and need has
already started out.
Never settle for second best,
You know where you need to go.

You and only you,
Are the biggest star in your show.

Run

Run with me to the ocean floor,
Somewhere far away we can explore.
Run with me to the silver moon and the glittery
skies,
So I can see their reflection perfectly in your
eyes.
Run with me to the forest trees,
So we can lay for a while and simply be,
A quiet place for you and me.
Run with me to the loudest place,
May this be our saving grace.
Hold me here.
Wherever we are oceans, forest, moon or stars,
Just walk with me so close by.
Let me look into your eyes,
Feel your body close to mine.
That full embrace that takes me away to promise
lands,
The place that finalized all our plans.
And more.

Your very own story

This life is yours you get to keep,
A story of you when you go to sleep.
Write your pages,
Play your character well,
Some days of laughter,
Some days of hell.
Whether you're weak or strong,
Dance everyday play your favourite songs.
This part was made just for you,
A perfectly written poem or two.
Look around take it all in,
The love story, friends and laughter never ends.
Write your pages,
Play your character well.
Some days full of laughter,
Some days full of hell.

Not today, Not ever

Life's not taking us down this time,
Day by day,
No song or rhyme.
We're not ready to give in,
Not soft enough to let it win.
We are strong you and me,
Too hard to break,
There's way to much at stake.
We will walk heads held high,
Hand in hand,
Side by side.
Throw us some more,
We can do it,
Face it head on,
We'll get through it.
Throw that curve ball,
Watch us grow,
We'll catch it head on
And then we will know.
We are tough you and me,
Test us again so the world can see.
We've got this!

Diversity

We don't have to be the same,
It's ok to just stay in your lane.
You are you and I am me,
I'm not bothered by the clothes you wear,
The way you speak,
Or the style of your hair,
We are very much different but all still the same,
We arrived here just trying to make our way.
I care not for the colour of your skin,
Your designer clothes,
Or if you fit in.
If you're kind, humble, patient and true,
We are the same me and you.
You speak your language so eloquently,
Hold yourself so admirably.
Your making your way, your living life.
All in it together whilst everyone strives.....
For perfection.
You can lean on me and take my hand,
We can make a million plans.
I'll pull you back,
Hold you down,
Pick you up and make the sun shine down.
Nothings off limits as far as the eye can see,
We've got eachother and a whole world to see.

Life doesn't come with instructions,
There are no golden rules,
I've got you and you've got me,
And we can do it all.

One chance

How do you ignore me?
Walk by like I'm not there?
How do you do that?
Pretend that I'm not here?
Whilst I sit here overwhelmed by tears,
Hoping you'll notice and reassure my fears.
Once we had everything but now it's all lost,
You threw it all out with one solid toss.
You get on with your day like you have not a
care in the world,
Meanwhile I sit here my whole life upside down.
You only have once chance,
Make sure you use it well,
Because only once will I allow you to make my
life a living hell.

My boy

People stare
With no idea what we prepared to get here
Everyday we wake again to see what today may
bring
Everyday we try to smile
With 999 on speed dial
The oxygen cylinder never to far
Our bag , our life packed in the car
Your lifeless body
Your breathless soul
Now it's over its time to go
Blue lights
Tears
Your pale face
No one can ever take your place
Still no answers
Still no grace
Lie after lie
Face after face
You're one in a million
You're my special boy
You're one in a million
You're not a toy
Time has passed
Time goes on

We've listened to all our favourite songs
Your brain is calm
Your brain is saved
Everything is going our way
One hot day
One day too many
It's back around like a recent memory
It will never leave
It will always be
A part of you internally
You're a miracle all of your own
This special little boy of mine
You're here to stay
A shining light
And you my little love
You shine so bright